MW00387695

Wineman-Marcus and Wohl

Introduction to Parents, School Personnel and Psychotherapists

There are many books aimed at the prevention of sexual abuse; few story books are geared for children that deal with the profound emotional aftermath. This book is unique because it offers the use of engaging animal protagonists, which allows the child to work through painful emotions in a less threatening and more effective manner.

Among the most universal issues for the sexually abused child are: the mixed feelings toward the abuser, the dread and wish to be loved, the difficulties of disclosing the abuse, the fear of being blamed and/or of not being believed. The effects frequently culminate in a sense of vulnerability, damaged self-esteem, guilt and faulty defenses against the feelings of being hurt. This can lead to a wide range of self-destructive behavior in childhood and adulthood.

This gentle, "child friendly" animal tale provides children with a story they can listen to again and again. Parents, psychotherapists and school professionals can use this book as a point of entry into complex feelings that the youngster, or any sexually abused person might frequently experience. Our hope is this book will help the child begin the process of healing, and gradual resumption of his or her healthy psychological development.

*Note: Please substitute male for female as needed and the identity of the abuser.

Dedicated to all the victims throughout the world.
Our wish for all to find healing.

Our forest looks like a place where everyone
lives together in peace and happiness.
But things aren't always
          what they seem...

Let me tell you about
          Mother Deer,
          Father Deer
          and their daughter Fawn.

Father and Mother Deer were always
very busy. Fawn did not have
many friends
and was often alone...

One day Fawn was chasing a butterfly
around the bottom of my tree.

"Hey down there," I called.
"You're making me dizzy.

Why don't you sit down
and talk to me awhile?"

"Nah, I don't want to."

"I'm bored. I wish Dad was home.
When he's home we have fun together."

Dad and I play the best games.
We pretend we are a king and queen.

We chase goblins and conquer mountains.
"We splash in the stream.

Dad says we are crossing the Great River
to reach the outer kingdom," Fawn said laughing.

During the summer,
Fawn visited often.
Then, in the early fall, she came running
over to my tree very excited;
her Dad said he would be home more often.

I was happy for her and told her to come
to see me when she had time

I didn't see Fawn all fall or winter. In the spring,
I flew over the forest looking for her. When I
found her she looked different:
dirty and as if nobody cared.

"Fawn, where have you been? I've missed you!"

"It's my father," she answered angrily and ran off.

I followed high above the trees
keeping an eye on her. Fawn was
butting heads with the young deer.
Then she started to tease
the biggest buck.

He was just about to beat her up,
when I swooped down and stopped the fight.

"What is going on here Fawn?
What has happened to you?" I asked.
Fawn stormed off without a word.

A few days later,
I found Fawn in the largest meadow
in the forest. She was kicking her legs
up and running wildly round and round.
I landed on a nearby tree and said hello.

"Go Away," Fawn snapped.

Every day I looked for her, and every day
I waited for her to tell me what was wrong.

Time passed...

Fawn stopped telling me
to go away and we
sat in silence together.

"Something happened
between you and
your dad. I know it
must have been bad,
because you stopped visiting me, " I said.

"I don't want you
to hate me,"
she cried.

I stroked her head
with my wing.

"When I didn't want to play
Dad made me. When I didn't want
to be left alone with Dad,
Mom made me stay with him.
She said I had to keep
Dad company."

"Dad played let's pretend games, but they weren't like the first ones.

Dad wanted me to be an ice queen who he chases and conquers. When he caught me, he said he was touching the ice queen to melt her. The games were exciting, but scary too.

Sometimes the touching felt a little good, but it also felt bad.

Other times it hurt."

"I have terrible dreams
of monsters grabbing me.

When I cry out,
Mom never comes. Dad does
and when he does he touches me.

So I've learned to lie against the cold ground
and be quiet."

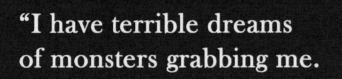

"Dad said never
tell our secret."

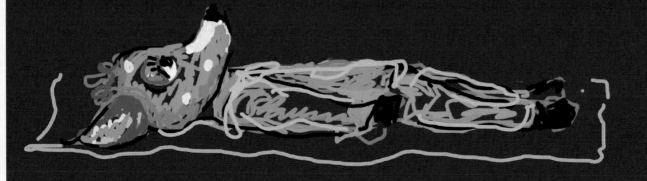

"I shouldn't have told. What will he do to me?
What's Mom going to say? She's going to be
mad at me."

Owls are wise but now I
had to be very wise.
"We must go to the
Willow Grove where
the Council of Elders meet.
You will tell them your story and they will help."

When we reached
the meeting place
Fawn told them
everything.

The Council spoke amongst themselves,
and then to Fawn.

"We believe your story. Now we must send
scouts to bring back your mother and father."

Fawn's mother was the first
to arrive.

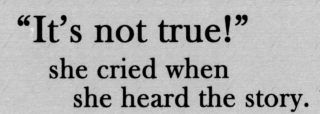

"It's not true!"
she cried when
she heard the story.

All through that day
Fawn's mother talked
with the Elders.

By nightfall she
admitted that in
her heart she knew
the story had
to be true.

The Elders spoke to Fawn's mother.

"You have not looked after your daughter.
You must try to understand how this
all happened without your knowing.

Then you must speak to your daughter
and hear what she is saying."

Fawn's father arrived the next day.

"I didn't do anything," he insisted
.
Fawn wished she'd said nothing.

But the Elders did not believe her father.

"Grown up deer must not play
    with little deer this way. You must go live
    on the far side of the forest."

"There you must get help for this
terrible problem. Then, in the future,
if we are sure you will not do this again,
    we might allow you back to this
    part of the forest," the Elders said.

To Fawn they said, "Whatever you thought
or wished, whether you liked the games
or hated them, it was not your fault.
You are not to blame."

All through the Spring and Summer,
Fawn and I met to talk. Fawn had
a lot to say after those terrible months
of silence.

"The other deer won't play with me. Before,
I would pick fights with the biggest deer.
Do you remember what you told me
about that?"

"You felt it was your fault...," I nodded.

"That's right. I wanted the bucks to hurt me
like they were punishing me
for what happened.
Now I know it was not my fault,
it was my father's fault," Fawn said.

Then Fawn ran to a group
of little deer who were playing nearby.
Although she didn't join them, she was gentle.

I could see she no longer wanted to hurt them
just to feel strong.

Later Fawn came back.
"I still don't know
how to make
them like me,"
    she said sadly.

"For you, being
close to
someone meant
getting hurt.
Playing with them
may be scary
because you don't
know when the hurt is going to come," I answered.

As the weeks passed, we kept meeting to talk.

Until one day, when Fawn said, "I've been
busy. I've joined in the games with the
        other deer. I run, jump and
            even laugh with them."

"Mom and I took a long walk. She said she was sorry for not protecting me and she knew I must feel angry and let down by her. Mom hoped that one day I could trust her again."

"Then we found some berries and ate them together."

Fawn's life looks normal now,
but I told you at the beginning,
things aren't always what they seem."

"Fawn is trying to understand why
she sometimes feels bad and
sad inside, even now
when everything
        is calm
    on the outside.

It's getting late, so this is the end of my story.
But it is not the end of Fawn's story.
She has her whole life to live.
Fawn knows there will be ups
and downs
but many happy times
lie ahead of her.

Text copyright ©2018
By Irene Wineman Marcus, Child & Adult Psychoanalyst
& Agnes Wohl, LCSW, ACSW
Jacket art and interior illustrations copyright ©2018
by Jackie Bluzer

Published by Stress Free Press

All rights reserved. This book or any portions thereof may not
be reproduced or used in any manner
whatsoever without the express written permission of the
publisher except for the use of quotations
in a book review.